This book belongs to

_____

YOU ALWAYS HAVE A FRIEND IN JESUS for Boys

JIM GEORGE

HARVEST HOUSE PUBLISHERS
EUGENE, OREGON

Cover by Dugan Design Group

Cover Photos © tomsaga / Fotolia; Inti St Clair / Alamy

YOU ALWAYS HAVE A FRIEND IN JESUS FOR BOYS
Copyright © 2016 Jim George
Published by Harvest House Publishers
Eugene, Oregon 97402
www.harvesthousepublishers.com

ISBN 978-0-7369-6417-3 (pbk.)
ISBN 978-0-7369-6418-0 (eBook)

Library of Congress Cataloging-in-Publication Data
Names: George, Jim, 1943- author.
Title: You always have a friend in Jesus for boys / Jim George.
Description: Eugene, Oregon, : Harvest House Publishers, 2016.
Identifiers: LCCN 2015041059 | ISBN 9780736964173 (pbk.)
Subjects: LCSH: Jesus Christ--Textbooks. | Boys--Religious life--Textbooks.
Classification: LCC BT207 .G465 2016 | DDC 248.8/2--dc23 LC record available at
https://lccn.loc.gov/2015041059

Printed in the United States of America

16 17 18 19 20 21 22 23 24 / VP-CD / 10 9 8 7 6 5 4 3 2 1

Contents

1

Jesus Is Your Friend

To say that Jesus was a special person is an understatement. That's why you won't read very far in the New Testament books of the Bible—especially Matthew, Mark, Luke, or John—before you discover that the stories of Jesus contain many lessons and show you character qualities about Jesus and His relationship with people. He treated people with kindness and helped many who were sick—even some who were dead!

Jesus was the greatest teacher who ever lived, and the greatest person who ever lived. His life, death, and being raised from the dead have transformed the lives of millions of people since He returned to heaven almost 2000 years ago.

"Yes," you agree, "Jesus is a special person, but what does this mean to me?" To begin to answer this question, think about this: This greatest of all people who have ever lived—Jesus Christ—wants to get to know you and become your friend. Look at what happened to some of the men who followed Jesus—to them He said:

I no longer call you servants, because a servant does not know his master's business. Instead, I have called you friends, for everything that I learned from my Father I have made known to you (John 15:15).

Can you think of some nice things that might happen if Jesus was your friend? List them here:

_____

_____

_____

Fun in God's Word!

It's always good to know the person who says he or she wants to be your friend. So let's take a few minutes and have some fun in God's Word as we get to know J-E-S-U-S.

Jesus is the Son of God. Many kids—and adults too—get confused when Jesus is called "the Son of God." They think this means that Jesus was not God, but was only God's Son, which makes them think Jesus is someone less than God. But read the verse below and answer this question: How did these people respond when Jesus said He was the Son of God?

For this reason [the Jews] tried all the more to kill him; not only was he breaking the Sabbath, but he was even calling God his own Father, making himself equal with God (John 5:18).

_____

_____

_____

According to John 20:31, what is the purpose of the Gospel of John, or the book of John?

These [things] are written [the words/messages in the Gospel of John] that you may believe that Jesus is the Messiah, the Son of God.

_____

_____

_____

According to the rest of John 20:31, what is the result of believing Jesus is the Son of God?

...that by believing you may have life in his name.

_____

_____

_____

Thomas, one of Jesus' disciples, heard Jesus say He was "the Son of God." He also heard others call Jesus by that title. What did Thomas call Jesus, knowing He was "the Son of God"?

Thomas answered and said to him, "My Lord and my God" (John 20:28).

_____

_____

Jesus is truly special because He is God who made heaven and earth. He created the first people on the earth, Adam and Eve. He had a special relationship with them, and now Jesus, who was God in human flesh, wants to be *your* friend. That's pretty cool, right? Actually, that's epic!

What else did Jesus do? Read on.

Entered this world as a baby. God is Spirit, which means He does not have a body. Since the time everything was created, God has wanted to have a personal relationship with the people He created. To make that possible, He had to become a man. Read the verses below and write out how God would become a man.

You [Mary] will be with child and give birth to a son, and you are to give him the name Jesus. He will be great and will be called the Son of the Most High. The Lord God will give him the throne of his father David, and he will reign over the house of Jacob forever; his kingdom will never end (Luke 1:32-33).

_____

_____

The angel promised Mary that a baby would be born. According to the verses below, where did the angel tell the shepherds they could find this very special baby?

Today in the town of David [Bethlehem] a Savior has been born to you; he is Christ the Lord. This will be a sign to you: You will find a boy wrapped in cloths and lying in a manger (Luke 1:11-12).

Once Jesus was born, He was God in a human body. He was a human person, like you and me. But He was also God, and He possessed all the qualities of God, which means Jesus possessed a perfect, sinless nature. He was and is 100 percent God and 100 percent man.

Sacrificed Himself for His friends. It takes a very special friend to be willing to die in your place. And yet that is what Jesus said He was willing to do for His friends. According to John 15:13, what is the proof of the greatest love in the world?

Greater love has no one than this: to lay down one's life for one's friends.

How did Jesus demonstrate His love for His friends—and you—according to Romans 5:8?

God demonstrates his own love for us in this: While we were still sinners, Christ died for us.

_____

_____

_____

Unites His friends with God's heavenly family. Jesus wants to be your friend, but with that friendship comes an additional relationship. What does God the Father want to do through your friendship with His Son?

God decided in advance to adopt us into his own family by bringing us to himself through Jesus Christ. This is what he wanted to do, and it gave him great pleasure (Ephesians 1:5 NLT).

_____

_____

_____

When you come into God's family through your friendship with Jesus, what gift does the Father give to you according to Galatians 4:6 (NLT)?

Because we are his children, God has sent the Spirit of his Son into our hearts, prompting us to call out, "Abba, Father."

When Jesus becomes your friend, He comes to live in your heart!

Secures eternal life for His friends. Jesus offers His friends a special kind of life—eternal life. "Eternal" means lasting forever—having no end. What do you have to do to receive eternal life, this life that has no ending?

God so loved the world that he gave his one and only Son, that whoever believes in him [Jesus] shall not perish but have eternal life (John 3:16).

Do you believe that Jesus is God and that He died for your sins? If so, God the Father wants you as a friend for His Son!

What a Friend You Have in Jesus!

Throughout this book you will read many stories from Jesus' life that are found in the Bible. They will help you understand that God came to this earth as a man so He could provide an opportunity for you to be His friend. Each chapter you read will show you how super special it is to be God's friend through His Son, Jesus.

Jesus Is Your Friend

In this chapter we had some fun in God's Word learning that **J-E-S-U-S** is God and **J-E-S-U-S** wants to have a personal relationship with you and be your friend. Think about how special your friend **J-E-S-U-S** is as you write out the points for each letter. (I'll get you started with "J.")

Jesus is the Son of God

E_____

S_____

U_____

S_____

Write out one thing you liked, learned, or want to do after discovering that Jesus wants to be your friend.

_____

_____

_____

_____

_____

A prayer to pray—

Jesus, it's hard to make a friend and to be a friend. Thank You for wanting to be my friend. Amen.

2

Jesus Is a Friend Who Loves at All Times

It's easy to love friends who return your love. Friendships are also easy to keep when you don't ask much from your friends. But what about times when you really need their help? Are they still there when you ask for their help? And what if that help is needed for a while, even a long while? The mark of a true friend is long-lasting love and care, regardless of any problems the friendship presents.

Many people think the word *love* has to do with emotional attraction to another person. But the Bible has another way of looking at love and measuring it. Furthermore, in the Bible we find the perfect person to demonstrate God's definition of love—Jesus Christ.

Fun in God's Word!

In this chapter we want to see how our friend Jesus practiced love. Because He was perfect, His love was perfect. Let's learn how to follow His example so that we can live out His command to *"love one another"* (John 13:34).

Jesus loved His friends. Can you imagine having Jesus in your home not only as an honored guest but also when you have a need? That's what happened in John 11 when Jesus' friend Lazarus became sick and died. You can read the full story of His visit to the home of three of His friends in John 11. What does John 11:5 say about Jesus' feeling toward these three friends?

Now Jesus loved Martha and her sister and Lazarus.

_____

_____

As a friend, Jesus' love for this family outweighed any concern He might have about His own safety. (At this time in His ministry, people were trying to kill Him.) A friend like Jesus loves even in difficult times.

Can you think of a time when you came to the aid of a friend? What did you do?

_____

_____

What will you do the next time you have a friend who is in need?

_____

_____

Jesus loved His fellow workers. What does this verse tell you about Jesus' relationship with His disciple, John?

One of them, the disciple whom Jesus loved [John], was reclining next to him (John 13:23).

What does this verse tell you about Jesus' feelings toward all of His disciples?

It was just before the Passover Festival. Jesus knew that the hour had come for him to leave this world and go to the Father. Having loved his own who were in the world, he loved them to the end (John 13:1).

It's easy to love your family and friends, but what about other kids at school? Jesus would want you to love them too! Is there a boy at school who isn't a close friend but one you could reach out to and show Jesus' kind of love? Put his name here:

What act of kindness could you do to show Jesus' kind of love to that person?

Jesus loved His enemies. Again, it's easy to love your family and friends. But what about those kids at school who give you a hard time? Maybe there's a bully at school or in your neighborhood. Maybe there's a group that won't let you join them. In Matthew 5:43, what did Jesus say you are to do?

I tell you, love your enemies and pray for those who persecute you.

How did Jesus respond to those people who nailed Him on the cross?

Father, forgive them, for they do not know what they are doing (Luke 23:34).

Most kids aren't really mean, and are not really the "enemy." Whatever you do, don't treat them the way they treat you. What does Jesus tell you to do instead?

Do to others as you would have them do to you (Luke 6:31).

Follow Jesus' advice and treat other kids the way you want them to treat you. Then see what happens!

Jesus loved you enough to die for you. What did Jesus do to show us what love is?

This is how we know what love is: Jesus Christ laid down his life for us (1 John 3:16).

_____

_____

God is love, and He showed us what love is by sending His beloved Son, Jesus. What was Jesus' mission when He came to earth?

God demonstrates his own love for us in this: While we were still sinners, Christ died for us (Romans 5:8).

_____

_____

Read John 1:12 below. What should be your response to the fact that Jesus loved you so much that He died to save you from your sins?

As many as received Him, to them He gave the right to become children of God, to those who believe in His name (NKJV).

_____

_____

In Jesus you will find both the greatest model of love and your ultimate resource for loving others. Jesus was perfect love in human flesh. He loves you perfectly, and He teaches—and commands—you to love others in the same way. Here's how your friend Jesus wants you to love: Circle the word "love" every time it is used in these verses:

Love—**chooses God as first and most important.** "*'You shall love the Lord your God with all your heart, with all your soul, and with all your mind.' This is the first and greatest commandment*" (Matthew 22:37-38).

Love—**chooses others as the next priority.** "*The second is like it: 'You shall love your neighbor as yourself'*" (verse 39).

Who is your neighbor? This same question was asked of Jesus, who explained that each of us is responsible to be a good neighbor to those who need our help (Luke 10:37).

Love—**chooses to obey Jesus.** "*If you love Me, keep My commandments*" (John 14:15 NKJV).

When Jesus said, "*keep My commandments,*" He was talking about following what the Bible says you and I should do. For example, you show Jesus that you love Him when you follow the Bible's command: "*Children, obey your parents*" (Ephesians 6:1).

Love—chooses to follow Jesus' command to love others. *"A new commandment I give to you, that you love one another; as I have loved you, that you also love one another"* (John 13:34).

When you refuse to like another person, you are not following Jesus' command. What does this say about your love for Jesus?

_____

Love—chooses to forgive rather than seek revenge. *"Love your enemies, bless those who curse you, do good to those who hate you, and pray for those who spitefully use you and persecute you"* (Matthew 5:43-44).

How do you usually respond when someone tries to hurt you?

_____

How should you respond, according to Jesus?

_____

Jesus Is a Friend Who Loves At All Times

In this chapter we have had some fun in God's Word. Look back at the four facts about Jesus' love for others, and write out the points that show you how Jesus loved others—including you!

Jesus loved His friends

J _____

J _____

J _____

Write out one thing you liked, learned, or want to do now after discovering that Jesus is a friend who loves at all times.

_____

_____

_____

_____

_____

_____

A prayer to pray—

Jesus, thanks for helping me know more about You and Your love. I really need help, especially with the kids who are mean or not so nice to me. Amen.

3

Jesus Is a Friend You Can Trust

Jesus was a great preacher and teacher—the greatest! While He was on earth, He spent His time moving from place to place throughout the small country of Judea. Jesus talked with lots of people and healed many who crossed His path. Eventually He chose 12 disciples to go with Him everywhere. As they moved about, Jesus taught the disciples and prepared them to continue His ministry after He returned to heaven.

These men were Jesus' friends. He protected them from the religious rulers who wanted to stop Him from telling people He was God, the Messiah and Savior of the world. Just before He was betrayed by Judas and the Roman soldiers, Jesus prayed this prayer:

> *While I was with them [the disciples], I protected them and kept them safe by that name you gave me. None has been lost except the one doomed to destruction so that Scripture would be fulfilled* (John 17:12).

How many of His friends did Jesus lose?

Even though at times the disciples didn't understand some of the things Jesus was saying, and even when they doubted Him, the disciples knew they could trust Jesus.

Fun in God's Word!

The disciples knew they could trust Jesus, and now it's time for you also to know that Jesus is a friend you can T-R-U-S-T.

Trust Jesus with your salvation. The disciples were kept under Jesus' protection while He was with them and He lost none of them, except Judas, who willfully betrayed Jesus. Like the disciples, you can fully trust Jesus and depend on Him for your eternal life. Write out these three promises that Jesus gave to His friends in John 10:28.

> *I give them eternal life,*
> *and they shall never perish;*
> *no one will snatch them out of my hand.*

Promise #1 _____

_____

Promise #2 _____

_____

Promise #3 _____

_____

According to John 10:29, who else is involved in making certain of your salvation besides Jesus?

> *My Father, who has given them [the disciples and Jesus' friends] to me, is greater than all; no one can snatch them out of my Father's hand.*

Remember, Jesus gives you a helper. Jesus knew His friends would have a hard time after He went back to heaven. After all, He was the one who had kept them safe, and they had relied on Him to lead them. So that they would not worry about His support in the future, Jesus promised to send "a helper" who would take His place. Circle the words in these verses that describe what this special "helper" does for Jesus' friends and followers:

> *I will ask the Father, and he will give you another Counselor to be with you forever—the Spirit of truth. The world cannot accept him, because it neither sees him nor knows him. But you know him, for he lives with you and will be in you* (John 14:16-17).

The disciples trusted that Jesus would keep His promise. And sure enough, in Acts 2:1-4, we learn that the Father sent the Holy Spirit to live in Jesus' friends and help them, just as Jesus had promised.

Understands your struggles. Do you ever get the feeling that no one understands what you are going through? You have your personal struggles and are tempted to say or do things that are wrong. Even your parents don't always understand. But your friend Jesus understands every single one of your struggles and temptations.

> We do not have a high priest [Jesus] who is unable to empathize with our weaknesses, but we have one who has been tempted in every way, just as we are—yet he did not sin (Hebrews 4:15).

Why is Jesus able to understand and help you with your problems?

_____

_____

According to Mark 1:13, how long did Jesus struggle with temptation when He began His ministry?

> He was in the wilderness forty days, being tempted by Satan (Mark 1:13).

_____

_____

When you face a struggle and are tempted to give up, remember that you can trust Jesus because He too was tempted and He knows exactly what you are going through. Since He knows your struggles, you can go to Him in prayer for help. Jesus "did not sin," which means He can help you work through your temptations and keep you from making the wrong decisions.

Speaks only the truth. Jesus was and is the truth. What three things does Jesus say about Himself in John 14:16?

> *Jesus answered, "I am the way and the truth and the life. No one comes to the Father except through me."*

1. Jesus said, "I am _____
2. and _____
3. and _____."

Why is it important to have a personal relationship with Jesus, according to the last part of verse 16?

_____

In one of the many times Jesus talked with the religious leaders about truth, He had the following to say about the devil. As you read along, circle the many bad qualities that describe the devil:

> *You belong to your father, the devil, and you want to carry out your father's desires. He was a murderer from the beginning, not holding to the truth, for there is no truth in him. When he lies, he speaks his native language, for he is a liar and the father of lies* (John 8:44-45).

List how the devil is opposite from Jesus when it comes to telling the truth:

_____

_____

Jesus is the truth, and He also wants His friends to tell the truth. What do these verses say you should always do?

Each of you must put off falsehood and speak truthfully to your neighbor (Ephesians 4:25).

_____

_____

[Be] speaking the truth in love (Ephesians 4:15).

_____

Jesus makes it very clear that those who are His friends should not lie. To believe in Jesus—who is the truth and spoke the truth—means that you will speak only the truth. Do you wish to please God and live—and speak—as His Son did? Then focus on living out this verse:

The LORD detests lying lips, but he delights in people who are trustworthy (Proverbs 12:22).

Thank Jesus for being trustworthy. Do you have a friend who is completely honest with you at all times? If you do, he is a rare friend indeed! Because Jesus is God, you can trust everything He says in His Word, the Bible. What does the following verse say comes through Jesus Christ?

The law was given through Moses; grace and truth came through Jesus Christ (John 1:17).

_____

Your friend Jesus is someone you can trust because when He speaks, He speaks the truth—always.

What a Friend You Have in Jesus!

Knowing that Jesus has reached out and wants to be your friend should help you trust Jesus, right? Jesus is God, and if you are one of His friends, He has promised to save and protect you. Because you can **T-R-U-S-T** Jesus, what response should you give back to Him? Let's use **T-R-U-S-T** for Proverbs 3:5-6 to give you a guide on how to respond.

> *Trust in the Lord with all your heart and do not lean on your own understanding. In all your ways acknowledge Him, and He will make your paths straight* (NASB).

Trust in the Lord—"Trust in the Lord with all your heart." God knows 100 percent of the time what is 100 percent best for you. He is the 100-percent-best person to trust with any decision you need to make.

Resist using your own understanding—"…and do not lean on your own understanding." Do you know everything there is to know in the world? No one does. Rather than try to do things by yourself with limited knowledge and understanding, lean on God's wisdom from His Word, the Bible. That is where you will find everything you need to know. And don't forget to ask your parents for help—they can provide wisdom too!

Understand His presence—"In all your ways acknowledge Him." Even though you cannot see Him, Jesus is always with you. Through prayer you acknowledge Him and His presence and can talk to Him about every decision you must make. How great is that? Jesus is always there by your side—at all times, night or day.

Straight paths come with God's help—"...and He will make your paths straight." God's job is to direct and guide you through life along a straight path. If you trust Him, He will clear the way for you so you can move onward in the right direction to do what is best for you and what pleases Him.

Take some time to make a choice—Maybe you have already chosen to trust Jesus with your salvation. But what if you haven't done that? Here is what you need to know: Jesus is the Son of God and is 100 percent holy and sinless. This presents a big problem because every single person is a sinner. As a result, every person is separated from God. (That's the bad news.) But the good news is that Jesus died on the cross for you. He took the punishment for your sins so you could be made right with His righteousness. If you accept Him by faith, you can have forgiveness for your sins.

According to Ephesians 1:7, two things happen when you put your faith and trust in Jesus. What are they?

In him [Jesus] we have redemption through his blood, the forgiveness of sins, in accordance with the riches of God's grace.

Happening #1 _____

_____

Happening #2 _____

_____

Jesus Is a Friend You Can Trust

In this chapter we had some fun in God's Word as we learned that we can **T-R-U-S-T** Jesus. On this page, write out the point for each letter. (I'll get you started with "T.")

Trust Jesus for your salvation

R_____

U_____

S_____

T_____

Write out one thing you liked, learned, or want to do now that you know you can trust your friend Jesus in all areas of your life.

_____

_____

_____

_____

_____

_____

A prayer to pray—

Jesus, I want to trust in You with all my heart. I want to make better decisions every day. I'm really glad You are my friend and will show me the right path. Amen.

4

Jesus Is a Friend Who Prays for You

It's impossible to read about the life of Jesus in the Gospels—in Matthew, Mark, Luke, and John—and not notice that He prayed a L-O-T. For Jesus, praying was like breathing. It was as if He couldn't live without praying. His one desire was to do what God, the Father, wanted Him to do. In His last recorded prayer to the Father before He went to the cross, Jesus said, *"I have brought you glory on earth by finishing the work you gave me to do"* (John 17:4).

How was Jesus able to finish the Father's work on earth? Prayer was a major tool He used for completing everything He was asked to do. Would you like to do everything God wants you to do? Well, prayer—as modeled by Jesus—is a big step toward knowing what you need to do.

Fun in God's Word!

If you borrowed one of your youth leader's books about Jesus and His life and ministry, that book would tell you that Jesus was a prophet, a priest, and a king. Right now in this book we want to look at Jesus' role as a priest, like that of an Old Testament priest. One of the functions of a priest in the

Old Testament was to pray for the people of Israel. This is what Jesus did for His friends as well—He prayed for them. Here are some facts about Jesus' prayers:

Jesus' prayers are continuous. Jesus spent His earthly ministry helping people and praying for them. After He was raised from the dead, He returned to heaven. What is Jesus doing in heaven right now for His friends—for *"those who come to God through him"*?

> *He is able to save completely those who come to God through him, because he always lives to intercede [pray for] them* (Hebrews 7:25).

_____

_____

Isn't it great that your friend Jesus is in heaven continually praying for you? That's what a friend does, and Jesus is concerned about His friends, including you. Think about your friends at school or on your ball team or at church—or even next door. Don't you think your friend Jesus would also want you to be praying for your friends here on earth? Write down the names of your best friends.

_____

_____

What can you be praying about for your friends? Jot down a few things, and begin to be a friend who prays.

_____

_____

_____

Jesus' prayers have authority. Do you know what authority is? Authority means you have the ability to make things happen. For example, your parents have authority, and so do your teachers and those who work in the government. But Jesus has the greatest of all authority! As God the Son, when He returned to heaven, He sat down at the Father's "right hand" (Hebrews 1:3), which is a position of power and authority. What does the Bible say Jesus is doing while He sits on His throne of authority?

> *There is one God and one mediator between God and mankind, the man Christ Jesus* (1 Timothy 2:5).

_____

_____

One thing a *mediator* does is to help explain to one person what is going on in another person's life. This is exactly what your friend Jesus is doing for you. With His authority as God's Son, Jesus is explaining to the Father that you are His friend and that He is personally helping you do the right things in your life.

Did you know that because you are a friend of Jesus you

have authority too? When you pray to God, what does Jesus say you are to do to get the Father's approval, and why?

> *I appointed you to go and produce lasting fruit, so that the Father will give you whatever you ask for, using my name* (John 15:16 NLT).

_____

_____

_____

When you pray using Jesus' name, you are asking God to consider your request in the same way He would respond to Jesus' own request. As a friend of Jesus, you have His authority behind you as you pray!

Jesus' prayers are for God's will. Read the following prayers from Jesus. What were some of the occasions for His prayers, according to these verses?

> *One of those days Jesus went out to a mountainside to pray, and spent the night praying to God. When morning came, he called his disciples to him and chose twelve of them* (Luke 6:12-13).

Here, Jesus prayed for God's will regarding

_____

_____

Simon, Simon, Satan has asked to sift all of you as wheat. But I have prayed for you, Simon, that your faith may not fail (Luke 22:31-32).

Here Jesus prayed for God's will that

_____

_____

Jesus was praying right before He was betrayed...He went away a second time and prayed, *"My Father, if it is not possible for this cup [of death] to be taken away unless I drink it, may your will be done"* (Matthew 26:42).

Here Jesus prayed for God's will regarding

_____

_____

Jesus did not want to do anything the Father didn't want Him to do. He wanted to do God's will. He prayed before choosing the disciples. He prayed that Simon Peter's faith would remain strong. And He prayed just before going to the cross so that God's will would be done.

At another time, Jesus told His disciples to make sure their prayers lined up with the Father's desires. Underline the last sentence of Jesus' instructions that tell you how to pray:

Pray like this:
    Our Father in heaven,

> *may your name be kept holy.*
> *May your Kingdom come soon.*
> *May your will be done on earth,*
> *   as it is in heaven* (Matthew 6:9-10 NLT).

Knowing "God's will" means you know what the Father wants you to do in your life.

What a Friend You Have in Jesus!

Your friend Jesus spent much of His life on earth praying for His friends. He also prayed for the Father to lead Him in doing what was necessary to ensure salvation for His friends. Today Jesus is in heaven praying for you at all times. His life of prayer shows you how you too can be praying for others.

But have you ever had times when you didn't know how you should pray? For example, suppose you are at church with other kids and the leader asks if anyone wants to pray. You would like to pray, but you are not sure what you should say. If so, you are not alone. Jesus' disciples had this same problem. They heard Jesus' prayers and watched Him pray to the Father. Finally they asked Jesus, "Lord, teach us to pray" (Luke 11:1). Here is a model prayer Jesus gave to His disciples, and He gives this same prayer to you too as a guide for your own prayers.

> *Father, may your name be kept holy.*
> *   May your Kingdom come soon.*
> *Give us each day the food we need,*
> *and forgive us our sins,*

as we forgive those who sin against us.
And don't let us yield to temptation (Luke 11:2-4 NLT).

Jesus' prayer can help guide you when you pray. But maybe you still don't quite understand how prayer works. Using the acrostic P-R-A-Y, let's learn more about how you can pray for yourself, your family, and your friends.

Prayer is talking to God. You have no problem talking to your parents or your friends, do you? The same ought to be true when it comes to talking to God. Read on and see what this verse says you need to do to get closer to God:

Draw near to God with a sincere heart (Hebrews 10:22).

What is it you are to do? _____

_____

What attitude should you have in your heart when you pray?

_____

Learning to talk to God is just like making friends. To make a friend, you need to take the first step and start talking to him or her. It's the same way with God. Take the first step and say, "Hello God, my name is _____. I want to be Your friend, and I have a few things I need to talk over with You." When you talk to God, be respectful, and be yourself—be sincere. God wants you to just be yourself—the real you—when you talk to Him.

Remember you must pray with a heart of faith. God has promised to answer your prayers, so you must believe that He will keep His promise. That's what faith is—believing what God says is true. Here's how you should pray:

> *Whatever you ask for in prayer, believe that you have received it, and it will be yours* (Mark 11:24).

What is your job or part in prayer?

_____

What does the verse above say will happen when you pray?

_____

Does this mean that you can ask and get anything you want, like a new bike or a video game? For help with the answer, look at the next verse.

> *When you ask, you do not receive, because you ask with wrong motives, that you may spend what you get on your pleasures* (James 4:3).

Ask, knowing that God promises to hear your prayers. Often we don't understand how God works. For some reason the God of the universe wants us to be a part of what He is doing in and around us. So when God promises us that He hears and answers our prayers, we need to start praying. Notice what God is promising to you when you A-S-K:

Ask and it will be given to you;

Seek and you will find;

Knock and the door will be opened to you (Matthew 7:7).

In the verse that follows, circle what you are to do and underline what God will do:

Call to me and I [God] will answer you and tell you great and unsearchable things you do not know (Jeremiah 33:3).

You need to confess sin before you pray. A big reason kids don't pray is because they have done something wrong and won't admit it. As a result, they are too embarrassed to talk to God. It's like not looking your parents in the eye because you know you did something you weren't supposed to do. (Like lying to them!) So, like with your parents, you need to admit the truth to God and tell Him you are sorry for what you did. You need to agree with God that what you did was wrong. Take a look at the next few verses, which talk about confessing your sin.

If I regard [sin] in my heart, the Lord will not hear (Psalm 66:18 NKJV).

What happens to your prayers when you sin and don't confess your wrongdoing to God?

_____

If we confess our sins, he is faithful and just and will forgive us our sins and purify us from all unrighteousness (1 John 1:9).

What happens when you confess your sin and admit it to God?

_____

_____

_____

Could you have any better friend than Jesus? Of course not. First, Jesus is always praying for you, day and night—when you are awake, and when you are asleep. Second, as you have seen in this chapter, your friend Jesus has given you guidance on how to pray for yourself and for others. Yes, Jesus is the greatest friend you can have!

In this chapter we had some fun in God's Word as we learned how your friend Jesus prays for you. And we have also learned what it means to **P-R-A-Y**. On this page, write out the points related to each letter in the word **P-R-A-Y**. (I'll get you started with "P.")

Prayer is talking to God

R _____

A _____

Y _____

Write out one thing you liked, learned, or want to do now after discovering that Jesus is a friend who prays for you all the time.

_____

_____

_____

_____

_____

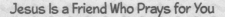

A prayer to pray—

I'm so glad You are a true friend I can talk to. I'm so glad You are there and You promise to listen to me when I pray. Amen.

5

Jesus Is a Friend
Whenever You Need Him

Most people all around the world, Christians and non-Christians, past and present, agree Jesus was a great person. Are you wondering, *What did Jesus do that caused so many people around the globe to acknowledge that He was the greatest man who ever lived?* Before we consider the answer, keep in mind what Jesus *didn't* do. As a man, He...

> never wrote a book.
>
> never commanded an army of soldiers or won great battles in war.
>
> never encouraged people to revolt.

Now let's look at what Jesus *did* do that made Him stand out above all others who ever lived. In a very few words, *He served others.* Jesus was aware and helped to meet people's needs, whether they were physical or spiritual.

And guess what? Jesus is still meeting the needs of His friends, as these verses declare:

...because Jesus lives forever, he has a permanent priesthood. Therefore he is able to save completely those who come to God through him, because he always lives to intercede for them. Such a high priest truly meets our need—one who is holy, blameless, pure, set apart from sinners, exalted above the heavens (Hebrews 7:24-26).

Fun in God's Word!

The first time that Jesus, God's Son and the Savior of the world, came to earth, it was as a lowly servant. As you read this chapter, open your heart and eyes and see how S-E-R-V-I-C-E was modeled by Jesus.

Serving describes Jesus' ministry on earth. In the two prophecies below that tell us about the first time Jesus came to earth, circle what the prophets called Jesus:

Here is my servant, whom I uphold, my chosen one in whom I delight (Isaiah 42:1).

See, my servant will act wisely; he will be raised and lifted up and highly exalted (Isaiah 52:13).

Evaluate who you are serving. The Bible tells us that very early in His ministry, Jesus was "tempted by the devil" (Matthew 4:1). In fact, He was tempted and tested for 40 days and 40 nights—and during that time, He went without food. The devil promised Jesus food and power and glory if He would fall down and worship and serve the devil. What did Jesus say in response to the devil (or Satan, as he is also called)?

Jesus said to him, "Away from me, Satan! For it is written: 'Worship the Lord your God, and serve him only'" (Matthew 4:10).

Jesus would not serve anyone other than God the Father. And He wants you to worship and serve the Father too. As we learned earlier, Jesus is God. With that in mind, who does Colossians 3:23-24 say you should also serve?

Whatever you do, do it heartily, as to the Lord and not to men, knowing that from the Lord you will receive the reward of the inheritance; for you serve the Lord Christ.

Remember what makes certain people special to God. Throughout the Bible you read about people who God used in a mighty way. Circle the name of each special person and underline why God chose to use these people.

I will bless you and will increase the number of your descendants for the sake of my servant Abraham (Genesis 26:24).

Why then were you not afraid to speak against my servant Moses? (Numbers 12:8).

By my servant David I will rescue my people Israel from the hand of the Philistines and from the hand of all their enemies (2 Samuel 3:18).

Would you like to be used by God in some special way? All you have to do is desire to be "a servant" of His. What does this mean? *A servant is a person who is devoted to or guided by someone or something.* Wouldn't you want to be devoted to and guided by God? If so, then you are on the right track to becoming a servant.

View serving God as your focus. Serving God is not easy. We have already seen that Jesus was tempted to serve something or someone other than God. Yet throughout His earthly life and ministry, Jesus kept His focus on the Father's will for His life. Jesus wants you to have that same focus. You would never knowingly want to serve Satan, but sometimes your service can focus on things that cause you to take your eyes off of God. In Jesus' day the religious leaders loved their worldly possessions, their things, their stuff. One day as they were listening to Jesus tell a story about a good servant (Luke 16:1-12), Jesus ended His story with this truth:

> *No one can serve two masters. Either you will hate the one and love the other, or you will be devoted to the one and despise the other. You cannot serve both God and money* (Luke 16:13).

The point of Jesus' story is that you need to be careful not to choose to serve something or someone other than God. Let me give you a few examples:

—Choosing to sleep a little longer, instead of getting up to read your Bible.

—Choosing to talk or draw pictures in church instead of listening to the Bible lesson.

—Choosing to spend all of your allowance on yourself and not give any at church.

Can you think of choices you can make that would help you to keep your focus on Jesus? Write your thoughts here:

_____

_____

_____

Imagine what serving others looks like. It's often said, "One picture is worth a thousand words." Well, in the Bible, John chapter 13 gives a very clear picture of what serving others looks like. Here is a part of that picture. Describe what Jesus did:

> *Jesus knew that the Father had put all things under his power, and that he had come from God and was returning to God; so he got up from the meal, took off his outer clothing, and wrapped a towel around his waist. After that, he poured water into a basin and began to wash his disciples' feet, drying them with the towel that was wrapped around him* (John 13:3-5).

_____

_____

_____

Normally in a dry and dusty land like Judea, a servant would wash the feet of the people who arrived for supper. But sadly, there were no servants present, and none of Jesus' disciples wanted to act like a servant and perform the lowly task of washing the dirty feet of others. So Jesus did what His disciples were not willing to do. Can you think of a time when you acted like a brat and chose not to be helpful when you could have acted like Jesus and helped out your mom or dad or your brother or sister at home?

_____

_____

What will you do next time you have an opportunity to serve?

_____

_____

Consider who Jesus wants you to serve. You already know that you should want to serve Jesus. According to the next two verses, who else does Jesus want you to serve?

You, my brothers and sisters, were called to be free. But do not use your freedom to indulge the flesh; rather, serve one another humbly in love (Galatians 5:13).

_____

_____

Sometimes it's hard to get excited about serving other people. But here's something to help you get excited about doing that. When you serve others, who is it you are really serving?

Serve wholeheartedly, as if you were serving the Lord, not people (Ephesians 6:7).

Examine how you are serving. When you serve, Jesus values not only your acts of service, but also the attitude you have when you serve. Name the two kinds of servants described in these two verses.

His master replied, "Well done, good and faithful servant! You have been faithful with a few things; I will put you in charge of many things. Come and share your master's happiness!" (Matthew 25:23).

His master replied, "You wicked, lazy servant! So you knew that I harvest where I have not sown and gather where I have not scattered seed?" (Matthew 25:26).

Be sure you notice that both the good and wicked people were servants. But the wicked servant was called "lazy," and the faithful servant was called "good." What does this tell you about how you should be serving God and others?

_____

_____

_____

Read Galatians 5:13 again—the verse under the letter C—
and write out how you are to serve others.

_____

Read Philippians 2:3-4. These verses talk about two attitudes you should not have as you serve.

*Do nothing out of selfish ambition or vain conceit [Pride].
Rather, in humility value others above yourselves, not looking to your own interests but each of you to the interests of
the others* (Philippians 2:3-4). What are the two attitudes
you should not have when you serve?

Wrong Attitude #1 _____

Wrong Attitude #2 _____

What attitude should you have instead?

Right Attitude _____

According to these verses, how do you know you are
serving with humility? Or, put another way, what are
the marks of humble service to others?

_____

_____

_____

_____

What a Friend You Have in Jesus!

Are you struggling with the idea of even wanting to serve? If so, start by deciding you will do something whenever you see a need or something that needs to be done. Decide you won't wait to see if someone else will do it. Make it a personal goal to volunteer to serve at home, at school, and in your youth class at church. Open your heart, your eyes, your hands—and serve.

Most of all, look to Jesus. He came to earth with a different lifestyle and a radical message of humility and service. Jesus defined true greatness as serving others, and then He lived out that definition. Jesus' mission was to serve others and to give His very life away—to die—for others. And that's exactly what He did.

Because Jesus is your friend and you are His friend, Jesus is asking and expecting you to follow His example—to be like Him. He wants you to develop a servant's heart and help others by taking care of their needs in the same way that Jesus, as your friend, is taking care of you.

In this chapter we had some fun in God's Word as we learned that Jesus was a servant the entire time He was on earth, and He wants us to follow His example. We spelled out **S-E-R-V-I-C-E** to help us understand what it means to serve. On this page, write out the point for each letter. (I'll get you started with "S.")

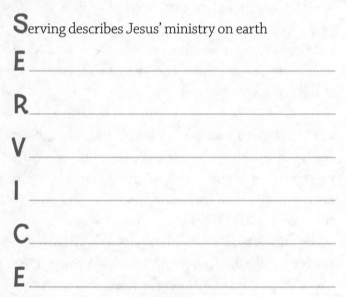

Serving describes Jesus' ministry on earth

E _____

R _____

V _____

I _____

C _____

E _____

Write out one thing you liked, learned, or want to do about serving others now that you know Jesus is your friend and helps you whenever you need Him.

_____

_____

6

Jesus Is a Friend Who Understands You

What are some of the best qualities you like about your close friends? I'm sure you could come up with a good list. And when you think about your best friend, one quality that probably stands out is that he knows and understands just about everything about you. He knows your favorite baseball team, your favorite hobby, your favorite flavor of ice cream...and the list could go on and on. When the two of you are together, it's like you are one person. You think alike and even talk alike. That's because you know and understand each other.

Well, your friend Jesus is that kind of friend too. He knows you inside and out like nobody else does, and He understands what's going on in your life. That's what makes Him such an amazing friend—because He knows you, He is aware of the times when you are hurting or in need.

As we read about Jesus' life as recorded in the Gospels, we notice that He had a special ability to know what people needed. It was like He was their closest and best friend. It's sort of like having a sixth sense or "people radar." Jesus had the ability to observe and notice when something was lacking or not quite right. He recognized when people had a need, and moved into action to help meet those needs.

How was Jesus able to know people's needs so well? Because He was God! And as we watch Him in action, we can discover how to observe other people's needs and do what is necessary to take care of those needs. Let's learn from Jesus as He walked among the people of His day.

Fun in God's Word!

In the last chapter we learned about S-E-R-V-I-C-E from the greatest servant of all, our friend Jesus. It was through serving that He met the needs of people. In this chapter we are going to learn more about how Jesus met other people's needs. In one word, Jesus was OBSERVANT.

To be observant means being aware of your surroundings. For example, when soldiers are trained for battle, they are told to be aware of their surroundings and to watch out for what might be lurking behind the next rock or tree. When police officers are trained, they are told to be aware of what is happening as they drive or walk the streets of their city. They are to watch everything around them carefully. And when your parents watch out for you and take care of you, they are also being observant. Sometimes you may even feel like they are able to read your mind! But what is really happening is that they are being observant.

Being observant and understanding is part of Jesus' nature. As God, He notices everything and everybody. And He also knows everything about you. By contrast, it's hard for us to be observant. Why? Because we are selfish. Rather than looking for ways to understand and help others, we are too busy thinking about our own needs.

Looking out for others and their needs is not easy. We have to train ourselves to be observant. We must develop the ability to notice when something is not right with a friend. Being observant will help you to recognize when something is wrong and your friend needs help. Let's go to the Bible and learn more about the ways Jesus was observant and understanding of others.

Jesus healed the sick. When Jesus was on the earth, there were no hospitals, and there were very few doctors and medicines. Many people who got sick ended up dying because nothing could be done for them. In the Bible, we read about many times when Jesus noticed people were sick. For example, one day He stopped at the home of His disciple Simon Peter, and helped a woman who was ill:

> *As soon as they left the synagogue, they went with James and John to the home of Simon and Andrew. Simon's mother-in-law was in bed with a fever, and they immediately told Jesus about her. So he went to her, took her hand and helped her up. The fever left her and she began to wait on them* (Mark 1:29-31).

Who was sick? _____

What did Jesus do? _____

_____

Usually physical illness is pretty easy to see. When one of your friends gets sick, you are able to tell because he looks really bad. You understand that your friend needs help, so you take him to the school office or tell your teacher about his need. Like Jesus, as a friend, you are there to help when someone has a physical problem.

Jesus had compassion for those who were hurting. Jesus also noticed those who were sad. Read about what happened one day when Jesus was approaching a city:

> As he approached the town gate, a dead person was being carried out—the only son of his mother, and she was a widow. And a large crowd from the town was with her. When the Lord saw her, his heart went out to her and he said, "Don't cry." Then he went up and touched the bier they were carrying him on, and the bearers stood still. He said, "Young man, I say to you, get up!" The dead man sat up and began to talk, and Jesus gave him back to his mother (Luke 7:11-15).

How can you tell that Jesus had compassion for the dead son's mother?

_____

_____

_____

When you observe people who have needs, the result should be compassion. In Luke 7:11-15, when Jesus saw the woman had lost her son, "his heart went out to her." To have compassion is another way of saying you feel sad for another person. You see someone hurting and you feel sad or bad for them. And if there is anything you can do, your sadness for them turns into action and you do what you can to help.

Jesus never refused to help anyone. With Jesus, there was never any prejudice. Jesus treated everyone the same—after all, He was the one who created everyone! One time Jesus and His disciples were on a journey and stopped in a place called Samaria. (You can read the full story in John 4.) The Jewish people did not like the Samaritans at all. They avoided the Samaritans and wanted nothing to do with them.

But that did not keep Jesus from talking to a Samaritan woman who came to the local well for water. He cared deeply about all people—even those who were different. He was observant and could tell the Samaritan woman had a need, and He reached out to her. How did Jesus' disciples react when they saw Him talking to the Samaritan woman?

Just then his disciples returned and were surprised to find him talking with a woman (John 4:27).

Are there any students in your school from other countries or from another state or city? Or maybe they are different in other ways. Jesus didn't care about where a person was from or that they looked or sounded or dressed differently. He was willing to help everyone. Can you think of a student at your school or in your neighborhood who is different and needs help? Write down something you could do next week to try and understand another person.

_____

_____

_____

Jesus loved the unpopular. It's easy to love people who love you and want to be your friend, or to love those who look, act, and dress like you. But what about those who are not like you? Most of the kids at school avoid those who are different or unpopular. They have no desire to understand or get to know them.

Would Jesus be like that? We both know the answer, don't we? No way would He avoid those who are different. In Luke 19:1-10, we read about the time Jesus met a man named Zacchaeus. This man was *the m-o-s-t* unpopular person in town because he was a tax collector. What did Jesus say and do when He noticed Zacchaeus sitting in a tree?

> *When Jesus reached the spot, he looked up and said to him, "Zacchaeus, come down immediately. I must stay at your house today." So he came down at once and welcomed him gladly* (Luke 19:5-6).

What did Jesus say and do? _____

_____

_____

What did Zacchaeus do? _____

_____

Now read about how the people around Jesus responded when they heard He was going to Zacchaeus's home:

All the people saw this and began to mutter, "He has gone to be the guest of a sinner" (Luke 19:7).

_____

Reaching out to those who are unpopular or different is not easy. Yet they need to meet Jesus just like Zacchaeus did. Jesus is not at your school—but you are. Your friend Jesus took notice of you, just like He took notice of Zacchaeus. Now it is time for you to take notice of others. When you do that, others may become upset with you, just like some people became upset with Jesus. But that should not matter to you as you follow Jesus' example. Can you think of someone at school or in your neighborhood or on your ball team you could approach this week and introduce yourself? Write their name here: _____

Jesus understood spiritual needs. Jesus had a mission to fulfill when He came to earth. What was that mission, according to Luke 19:10?

The Son of Man came to seek and to save the lost.

_____

According to this next verse, how did Jesus describe lost people?

When he saw the crowds, he had compassion on them, because they were harassed and helpless, like sheep without a shepherd (Matthew 9:36).

_____

_____

What did Jesus tell His disciples was needed to help these people who had no shepherd?

Then he said to his disciples, "The harvest is plentiful but the workers are few. Ask the Lord of the harvest, therefore, to send out workers into his harvest field" (Matthew 9:37-38).

_____

_____

In Matthew 9:37-38, Jesus was telling the disciples that they and others needed to be like "workers" who harvest crops, and help people who are lost and need to know about Jesus. As you read Luke 7:34, notice and underline how Jesus encourages you to approach those who are lost and in need of a Savior.

The Son of Man [was]...a friend of tax collectors and sinners.

What is God's message of love and hope for lost people both then and now, according to John 3:16?

God so loved the world that he gave his one and only Son, that
whoever believes in him shall not perish but have eternal life.

Your friend Jesus spent His earthly ministry helping people get to know God. He understood their spiritual needs and He cared about them. You can follow in His footsteps by looking around for those who are hurting and sad. Are there kids you know who are like sheep who have no shepherd? These are the kids you can introduce to your friend Jesus. They are spiritually lost, and Jesus can help them find eternal life.

What a Friend You Have in Jesus!

Over and over again Jesus observed the needs of others and was willing to take the first step to reach out and help them. Many people came to Jesus for aid, and He was available and helpful to them. He even went looking for those who needed His helping hand and His words of encouragement. And guess what? Jesus is looking out for *you* today. He is observing you and sees your needs and is providing for them. How is He doing that?

He has given you parents who take care of your physical needs.

He has given you teachers at your church to care for your spiritual needs.

He has given you the Bible as an instruction book on how to act. And best of all, as your friend...

He has given you His Spirit to help you act like Him every day of your life.

Again, you have to say, "What a friend I have in Jesus!"

Jesus Is a Friend Who Understands You

In this chapter we had some fun in God's Word as we learned that Jesus was **OBSERVANT**. He paid attention to the needs of others the whole time He lived on earth, and we should want to follow His example. To help you understand what it means to observe the needs of others, write out the points made in this chapter. I'll get you started with #1.

Jesus healed the sick

J_____

J_____

J_____

J_____

Write out one thing you liked, learned, or want to do about seeing Jesus care about others and become their friend.

_____

_____

_____

_____

_____

A prayer to pray—

Dear Jesus, help me be a true friend to others, to be more aware and caring of those in need. Please give me the love and courage to act and help them in whatever ways I can. Amen.

7

Jesus Is a Friend Who Is Gracious

Jesus. Just say His name, and the word *grace* probably comes into your mind. Jesus was the most gracious, giving, generous person who ever lived. Aren't you glad He extended the marvelous grace of His salvation to sinners like you and me?

In our culture today, a gracious person is someone who shows respect, honor, and kindness to others. As we look at Jesus, we see that He showed a kind attitude to all people. This same kind, respectful attitude is what Jesus wants you to pass on to others—as you meet and talk with your friends, as you address your teachers and other adults, and especially when you speak to and interact with your parents.

Fun in God's Word!

In this chapter we want to see how our friend Jesus practiced gracious and kind behavior. Because Jesus was perfect, He is a good example to follow. His kind actions show us how to live out His command that we "be kind...to one another" (Ephesians 4:32).

Jesus was gracious with His words. Jesus was a teacher, and a teacher must teach. What happened in Jesus' hometown on one occasion, according to Luke 4:16?

> *He [Jesus] went to Nazareth, where he had been brought up, and on the Sabbath day he went into the synagogue, as was his custom. He stood up to read...*

_____

_____

After reading from the Scriptures, Jesus sat down to teach His listeners the meaning of the verses He had read. What was the response of those who heard Jesus teach (verse 22)?

> *All spoke well of him and were amazed at the gracious words that came from his lips.*

_____

_____

Jesus was known both for His words of kindness and His wisdom. He did not use phony flattery or exaggeration. Today you represent Jesus to those around you. How would you describe your speech toward your family and friends? Here is a list of words that describe how people speak to others.

kindly   respectfully   disrespectfully
uncaring   caring   hurtful

Pick the words that describe how you normally speak to others. You can use each word as many times as needed to describe how you usually speak to...

Friends? _____

Teachers? _____

Other students? _____

Your brothers and sisters? _____

Your parents? _____

If you are honest with yourself, maybe you have come to realize you haven't been as gracious and kind with your words as you should be. That's why this lesson about being kind and gracious should be helpful.

An additional thought: A gracious person will say "Please" and "Thank you." Are you a gracious person? If not, what's missing? What changes should you make right away?

_____

_____

Jesus was gracious with people. Have you ever been around someone who made a mistake and another person was very quick to point out their mistake in front of others? They may even describe that person using terrible names like "idiot" or "stupid" or "dummy." Maybe you were the one who received the name-calling. Hopefully you were not the one calling other people those names!

Read this story found in Luke 10:38-42, when Jesus and His 12 disciples were visiting His friends Mary, Martha, and Lazarus. Martha was upset because her sister Mary was not helping her in the kitchen. Instead, Mary was listening to Jesus in another room. Rather than scold Martha or speak harshly to her, Jesus said,

> *Martha, Martha...you are worried and upset about many things, but few things are needed—or indeed only one. Mary has chosen what is better, and it will not be taken away from her* (verses 41-42).

Jesus wanted to gently show Martha that her real priority, her Number One priority—"what is better"—was to sit and hear His teaching.

Jesus was sitting right in Martha's house! And she was missing out on knowing, hearing, and worshipping Him. Yet Jesus didn't scold or put her down—He graciously taught her and reminded her that her focus was on her work instead of her worship. What do you want to remember from Jesus' response to Martha the next time someone makes a mistake or does the wrong thing?

_____

_____

_____

Jesus was kind to people. There is no record in the Bible of Jesus ever refusing anyone who approached Him for help. One wonderful example of how Jesus responded to people appears in Matthew 20:31-34. There, we read that two blind beggars called out to Jesus as He was making His way toward Jerusalem during the last week of His life here on earth. How did the crowd treat the blind men?

> *The crowd rebuked them and told them to be quiet, but they shouted all the louder, "Lord, Son of David, have mercy on us!"* (verse 31).

_____

_____

These blind men were told by the crowd to stay quiet, to quit calling out to Jesus as He passed by. After all, Jesus was on His way to Jerusalem and He had important things to take care of. But read the next few verses, and make a list of what Jesus did.

> *Jesus stopped and called them. "What do you want me to do for you?" he asked. "Lord," they answered, "we want our sight." Jesus had compassion on them and touched their eyes. Immediately they received their sight and followed him* (verses: 32-34).

Jesus _____

Jesus _____

Jesus _____

Do you want to follow Jesus' example and be gracious and show kindness to others? Start by going to your parents and asking them, "How can I help you today?" Then write down how you were able to help.

_____

_____

_____

Jesus showed kindness through His touch. When you think of a kind or gracious person, what one act usually shows that person's concern? It's a touch, right? Maybe a hug. A pat on the back. Even a fist-bump or a high-five. Jesus healed many people. Describe what Jesus did in each of these scenes:

Once more Jesus put his hands on the man's eyes. Then his eyes were opened, his sight was restored, and he saw everything clearly (Mark 8:26).

_____

_____

Jesus reached out his hand and touched the man. "I am willing," he said. "Be clean!" And immediately the leprosy left him (Luke 5:13).

_____

He went up and touched the [coffin] they were carrying [the dead man] on, and the bearers stood still. He said, "Young man, I say to you, get up!" The dead man sat up and began to talk, and Jesus gave him back to his mother (Luke 7:14-15).

The next time a brother or sister or even your mom, dad, or a friend seems to be having a bad day, try following Jesus' example and reach out and touch them. You don't even have to say a word. They will know by a simple touch that you care.

Jesus was gracious to outsiders. Many of the Jewish people in Jesus' day were very private and proud of themselves. They didn't want anything to do with anyone who did not look or act like them. Read on and write out what Jesus did when He met people who were "outsiders" in the eyes of the Jewish nation.

Jesus said to the centurion [a Gentile soldier], "Go! Let it be done just as you believed it would." And his servant was healed at that moment (Matthew 8:13).

The woman was a Greek, born in Syrian Phoenicia. She begged Jesus to drive the demon out of her daughter...Then he told her, "For such a reply, you may go; the demon has left your daughter" (Mark 7:26,29-30).

When a Samaritan woman came to draw water, Jesus said to her, "Will you give me a drink?" (John 4:7-8).

In these verses and many more, Jesus was kind and gracious in spite of the fact these people were different and were outsiders to His own group. Write down what you can do this next week when you come in contact with those who are considered "outsiders" by others, even by your friends.

What a Friend You Have in Jesus!

Jesus was perfectly gracious. Because of His love, He was warm, courteous, and kind. He didn't just turn on graciousness when needed—and then just as easily turn it off. No, Jesus was gracious in nature. He was genuinely gracious all the time.

And guess what? Jesus hasn't changed since His time on

this earth. He is still that warm kind person who wants to be your friend. He is now asking *you* to have this same attitude—*His* attitude—toward others. You do this when your heart is filled with His love and your mouth speaks with gracious words. The result? People will feel welcome and cared for when they are around you.

And best of all, your graciousness and kindness will draw people to Jesus.

Jesus Is a Friend Who Is Gracious

In this chapter we have had some fun in God's Word. Review again how special your friend Jesus is as you write out the points that show how Jesus was **gracious** and kind to others.

Jesus was gracious with His words.

J _____

J _____

J _____

J _____

Write out one thing you liked, learned, or want to do about discovering that Jesus is a friend who treats people with grace and kindness.

_____

_____

_____

_____

_____

_____

A prayer to pray—

Gracious Lord, thank You for the wonderful grace You show toward me every single day. You have set a great example for me. Please help me remember to be gracious to others and extend Your grace to them. Amen.

8

Jesus Is a Friend Who Is Generous

Do you receive an allowance from your parents, or maybe do chores to earn money? If you do, you probably know how easy it is to spend that money on yourself and how hard it is to give it to others.

Well, your friend Jesus is an awesome model of generosity and unselfishness. To begin the list of what He has so generously given, consider that He gave up His place of honor in heaven to become human. This does not mean He gave up His eternal powers; rather, it means He chose to live in obedience to the Father's will on earth. "He became poor" when He became human because He sacrificed so much (2 Corinthians 8:9).

In fact, Jesus explained that "foxes have dens and birds have nests, but the Son of Man has no place to lay his head" (Matthew 8:20). Jesus' sacrifice and generosity in giving up everything, including the comforts of a home, was so that "you through His poverty might become rich" through receiving His free gift of salvation and eternal life (2 Corinthians 8:9).

Now that you know this, it's easy to understand that

generosity, as defined by the life and character of Jesus, means sacrificial giving. Let's look at Jesus' life on this earth to get an idea of how we can follow His actions. But beware! After this study, you may need to turn the level of your generosity way up, even all the way into the range of sacrificing a few things.

Fun in God's Word!

In this chapter we want to see how Jesus practiced generous behavior. Because Jesus was perfect, His actions show us exactly how to be generous. Each point that follows explains more about being generous and starts with the word GIVING.

Giving was first demonstrated by God the Father.

Throughout the Old Testament, from Genesis to Malachi, God is seen as a generous, loving, giving God. For example...

God gave life to Adam and Eve.

God gave safety and salvation to Noah and his family during the Flood.

God gave manna to sustain His chosen people in the wilderness.

God gave the Promised Land to His people for a home.

God gave David the promise of a future king, a Savior who would redeem man from his sin.

God gave His prophets visions of a coming Savior, His very own beloved Son.

God gave His only begotten Son, Jesus.

Giving was modeled by the Son. Without question, Jesus is the ultimate model of giving, for He gave the ultimate gift in the sacrifice of Himself—in death—to forgive our sins and secure eternal life for us. What do you learn about Jesus and what He willingly gave?

> *The Son of Man did not come to be served, but to serve, and to give his life as a ransom for many* (Matthew 20:28).

_____

_____

Giving should be done with the right attitude. You remember what many call "the Christmas story" in the Bible, right? The wise men traveled a long distance to worship the child Jesus and bring their gifts to Him. What attitude did the wise men show as they presented their gifts to Jesus?

> *On coming to the house, they saw the child with his mother Mary, and they bowed down and worshiped him. Then they opened their treasures and presented him with gifts of gold, frankincense and myrrh* (Matthew 2:11).

_____

_____

Now read 2 Corinthians 9:7 below to learn what the apostle Paul wrote about giving and the kind of heart attitude you should have as you give "gifts" to God.

> *Each of you should give what you have decided in your heart*

to give, not reluctantly or under compulsion, for God loves a cheerful giver (2 Corinthians 9:7).

Your giving should not be...

_____

_____

Your giving should be with a _____ heart. What is God's response to those who give with the right heart attitude?

_____

In the verse that follows, what do you discover about Jesus' attitude as He gave His life as a sacrifice for sin?

For the joy set before him he endured the cross, scorning its shame, and sat down at the right hand of the throne of God (Hebrews 12:2).

_____

Jesus willingly, joyfully gave Himself as a sacrifice for sin—your sin. Knowing that God loves a cheerful giver, what should be your attitude when it is time to give back to God?

_____

_____

_____

_____

Giving has nothing to do with how much you have. Jesus pointed out this truth through the actions of an amazing woman. Read her story below:

> *Jesus sat down opposite the place where the offerings were put and watched the crowd putting their money into the temple treasury. Many rich people threw in large amounts. But a poor widow came and put in two very small copper coins, worth only a few cents.*
>
> *Calling his disciples to him, Jesus said, "Truly I tell you, this poor widow has put more into the treasury than all the others. They all gave out of their wealth; but she, out of her poverty, put in everything—all she had to live on"* (Mark 12:41-44).

How much money did the rich people give? _____

_____

How much money did the poor widow give?

_____

Who gave the most, the rich people or the widow, and why?

_____

Jesus explained that the widow gave more than all the others. How was that possible? Because the others *"gave out of their wealth"* at little personal cost and sacrifice, while the widow gave *"out of her poverty."* In comparison, she had given the most—she gave everything that she had to live on!

Jesus also gave all that He had—His life. What one thing

can you do this week to follow the example set by Jesus and the widow? (This would be a good thing to talk about with your parents.)

_____

_____

Remember, it's not *what you have* that's important, but *what you are willing to give* that's important to God!

Giving shows where your heart is. Giving is a matter of the heart. The Pharisees, a group of religious leaders in Jesus' day, made a great show of giving to the poor. However, Jesus taught that people should do just the opposite when they gave generously. How did He say giving should be done, according to Matthew 6:3-4?

> *When you give to the needy, do not let your left hand know what your right hand is doing, so that your giving may be in secret.*

_____

Giving God's way shows what is really in your heart because you are giving to God and making sure no one else knows what you are giving. What result is mentioned in verse 4?

> *Then your Father, who sees what is done in secret, will reward you* (verse 4).

_____

Giving provides a savings account in heaven. When I was younger, my dad encouraged me to put money in a local bank. I faithfully did this for years. As you can imagine, I was really counting on that money. With it I would be able to buy all sorts of stuff! Unfortunately, something happened and I lost all my savings. In His famous Sermon on the Mount, Jesus described how this same thing can happen to anyone, including you:

> *Do not store up for yourselves treasures on earth, where moths and vermin destroy, and where thieves break in and steal. But store up for yourselves treasures in heaven, where moths and vermin do not destroy, and where thieves do not break in and steal. For where your treasure is, there your heart will be also* (Matthew 6:19-21).

When it comes to giving, what do you think Jesus meant by this last statement: *"For where your treasure is, there your heart will be also"* (verse 21)?

_____

_____

_____

Verse 21 is a key principle to remember and memorize. It points out that whatever occupies your thoughts and time is where your affections—your heart—will be.

Giving isn't always about money. In Luke 10:29-36, Jesus told a story about a man who was robbed and beaten while on a journey. Two people who passed by the beaten man did not stop to give him any help. But a third man stopped. What did he do for the wounded man?

He went to him and bandaged his wounds, pouring on oil and wine. Then he put the man on his own donkey, brought him to an inn and took care of him (verse 34).

_____

_____

_____

_____

You may not have much money to give to the needs of others right now, but you can be a giver by offering a helping hand—to your mom and dad and brothers and sisters around the house, or to a friend who is having a hard time. It will only cost you your time—but what a gift!

What a Friend You Have in Jesus!

Can you imagine having everything and yet being willing to give it all up? That's exactly what Jesus did, which proves how much your friend Jesus loves you: *"Greater love has no one than this: to lay down one's life for one's friends"* (John 15:13). If you want to be like Jesus, then giving is a must. No one can out-give God, but if you are Jesus' friend, you should want to follow His example and give to God's work and for the needs of others. As Jesus told His disciples and now is telling you, *"Freely you have received; freely give"* (Matthew 10:8).

A good place to start giving is at home. At your age you might not have much money, but there are other ways you can give. For example, you can give the gift of obedience to your parents. Each day, see yourself as offering up your life to serve Jesus by doing what your parents want you to do. In fact, God commands, *"Children, obey your parents in the Lord, for this is right"* (Ephesians 6:1). And make sure you do this with the right attitude. Also, don't forget to be a giver to your brothers and sisters. Everyone needs some help and encouragement.

Jesus Is a Friend Who Is Generous

In this chapter we have had some fun in God's Word. Review again how special your friend Jesus is as you write out the points that show you how **generous** He was to others. Here's an example:

Giving was first demonstrated by God the Father

G_____

G_____

G_____

G_____

G_____

G_____

Write out one thing you liked, learned, or want to do after discovering that Jesus is a friend who is generous.

_____

_____

_____

_____

A prayer to pray—

Lord Jesus, thank You that You gave the best gift of all when You sacrificed Yourself to pay for my sins. May I become a generous giver like You. Amen.

9

Jesus Is a Friend Who Is Faithful

You probably won't meet very many people who are truly faithful. Something in us wants to be lazy, do it later, wait a little longer, or take a shortcut. But this was not so with Jesus!

Jesus was faithful to God's purpose. He came to earth for a reason, declaring, *"My food...is to do the will of him who sent me and to finish his work"* (John 4:34). Jesus' work was to live and die as the perfect sacrifice for man's sin.

But as Jesus went about doing good and feeding the multitudes who followed Him, His followers grew into a multitude of thousands. The people had a different purpose in mind for Jesus, especially after they witnessed Him feeding 5000-plus men and probably their families as well. They wanted Jesus to be their leader and to provide food for them on a regular basis. (You can read the full story in John 6:22-33.)

But despite many distractions and the desires and demands of the people, Jesus was faithful to God's plan and told the crowds, *"I have come down from heaven not to do my* will [or, by the way, the will of the crowd] but to do the will of him who sent me" (John 6:38).

Fun in God's Word!

Faithfully following Jesus will require you to ask the question, "Am I willing to listen to Jesus and not to 'them'— to the voices of my friends, to other students at school or kids in my neighborhood, to the popular people, to TV, magazines, and the words in music?"

If you haven't already made a commitment to be loyal to Jesus, it's time. You can do this by saying in your heart, "Jesus, I am willing to follow in Your steps and be faithful regardless of what others may say or do to me."

To help you with your commitment to being faithful, we will use the word FAITHFULNESS in this chapter to show how your friend Jesus was faithful in all things.

Faithfulness starts with God, the Father. The Bible speaks of God's faithfulness. Write out what these verses say about God's faithfulness.

Because of the LORD's great love we are not consumed, for his compassions never fail. They are new every morning; great is your faithfulness (Lamentations 3:23).

_____

_____

Great is your love, reaching to the heavens; your faithfulness reaches to the skies (Psalm 57:10).

Here are a few more ways God has shown His great faithfulness:

> He was faithful to provide coverings for Adam and Eve after their disobedience (Genesis 3:21).
>
> He was faithful to promise a Savior (Genesis 3:15).
>
> He was faithful to expand on His initial promise to send a Savior (Isaiah 9:6).
>
> He was faithful in fulfilling His promise as Jesus, God's only Son, was born as Savior (Luke 2:11).
>
> He was faithful in providing a divine model of His very nature through the life and ministry of Jesus as He walked among us as God in human flesh (John 1:14).

Faithfulness is modeled by the Son. To the very end of His life, day by day Jesus faithfully moved toward the purpose God set for Him. On the night before His death, Jesus declared His faithfulness to the Father. How faithful was Jesus in completing His mission?

> *I have brought you glory on earth by finishing the work you gave me to do* (John 17:4).

What tasks have your parents asked you to do this week? Write them here:

_____

_____

_____

_____

Now check the ones to which you can say, "I have finished the work that was given to me."

Faithfulness was seen in Jesus' prayers. Jesus was also faithful in prayer, or talking with God the Father. Prayer was a key way Jesus communicated with the Father and received His Father's direction. What did Jesus do in the middle of a very busy life?

> *Very early in the morning, while it was still dark, Jesus got up, left the house and went off to a solitary place, where he prayed* (Mark 1:35).

_____

What did Jesus do when He had a big decision to make?

> *Jesus went out to a mountainside to pray, and spent the night praying to God. When morning came, he called his disciples to him and chose twelve of them, whom he also designated apostles* (Luke 6:12-13).

_____

What did Jesus do when He was concerned that His disciples were under spiritual attack from Satan?

Simon, Simon, Satan has asked to sift all of you as wheat. But I have prayed for you, Simon, that your faith may not fail (Luke 22:31).

What is Jesus doing right now in heaven?

Christ Jesus who died—more than that, who was raised to life—is at the right hand of God and is also interceding [praying] for us (Romans 8:34).

Jesus was faithful to pray when He was on earth, and even now while He is in heaven He is faithfully praying for you. What does Jesus' example of being faithful in prayer teach you about being faithful to pray?

Faithfulness is a sign of devotion. Can you imagine what Jesus' last day was like—the day He was nailed to the cross? It was the most horrible day ever on earth. Yet a loyal band of women who often traveled with Jesus and supported Him in many ways were present with Him the day of His crucifixion and death. These women stayed with Him even at the foot of the cross. They were faithful to the end, while Jesus' own disciples could not handle what was happening. They all fled, except for John. What do you see the faithful group of women doing on the third day after Jesus' death?

> When the Sabbath was over, Mary Magdalene, Mary the mother of James, and Salome brought spices so that they might go to anoint Jesus' body. Very early on the first day of the week, just after sunrise, they were on their way to the tomb (Mark 16:1-2).

_____

_____

Even though these women had seen a great tragedy and were in grave danger, they were faithful to the end, bringing spices to properly prepare Jesus' body for burial.

How does the faithful devotion of these women encourage you to be faithful in your devotion to Jesus?

_____

_____

_____

Faithfulness was part of Jesus' ministry to His disciples. Jesus was faithful to protect His disciples while He was physically with them. What prayer request did Jesus make to the Father on the night before His death?

None has been lost except the one doomed to destruction [Judas] so that Scripture would be fulfilled (John 17:12).

Jesus' promise to protect His disciples continues on for you and for all who put their faith and trust in Him. Underline each promise Jesus made in John 10:28-29 about keeping you safe.

I give them eternal life, and they shall never perish; no one will snatch them out of my hand.

My Father, who has given them to me, is greater than all; no one can snatch them out of my Father's hand.

Take a moment to offer up a silent prayer of thanks to Jesus for faithfully keeping watch over you.

Faithfulness begins with family. Jesus was faithful to His family. Loyalty is a rare quality, whether today or in Jesus' day. What does this verse tell you about Jesus' commitment to His family at age 12?

He went down to Nazareth with them [His parents] and was obedient to them (Luke 2:51).

Even at the end of His life, Jesus was faithful to respect and watch over Mary, His mother. Looking down from the cross upon His mother and His disciple John, He asked John to take care of Mary. In a few words, what did John do according to John 19:26-27?

When Jesus saw his mother there, and the disciple whom he loved standing nearby, he said to her, "Woman, here is your son," and to the disciple, "Here is your mother." From that time on, this disciple took her into his home.

Obeying your parents is an act of faithfulness. In fact, it is a command from the Lord—*"Children, obey your parents in the Lord, for this is right"* (Ephesians 6:1).

What a Friend You Have in Jesus!

As a young man who is a Christian, it is vital that faithfulness be a quality that describes you and shines brightly in your life. When you are faithful, you show that you are born of God and belong to Him through His Son. Jesus had a heart for faithfully doing the Father's will. He was also faithful to His disciples and family and others, and He faithfully prayed for them. And now He is faithfully praying for and caring for *you*, His friend.

As you walk in faithfulness, you mirror the heart of your steadfast Savior. You also bear fruit that shows Christ lives within you. Your family is blessed when they can depend on you and trust you.

In this chapter we have looked at many instances of Jesus' faithfulness. The good news is you can develop the same faithfulness Jesus showed. You can grow in faithfulness that follows through, fulfills your responsibilities, shows up, and keeps your word and your commitments.

If this sounds impossible or like a hard uphill climb, take Step One: Call upon God in prayer. And then start small—in the little things. Count on Jesus' strength. In Him you can do all things, including being faithful (Philippians 4:13). Also ask God for His help to work at getting rid of laziness and fulfilling this major purpose He has for you—that you would be *faithful in all things* (1 Timothy 3:11 NKJV).

Jesus Is a Friend Who Is Faithful

In this chapter we have had some fun in God's Word. Review again how special your friend Jesus is as you write out the points that show us about Jesus' **FAITHFULNESS**.

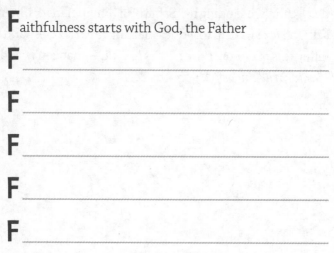

Faithfulness starts with God, the Father

F _____

F _____

F _____

F _____

F _____

Write out one thing you liked, learned, or want to do about discovering that Jesus is a friend who is faithful.

_____

_____

_____

_____

_____

A prayer to pray—

Lord Jesus, help me day by day to be faithful like You are. I want to do what I say I will do. I want to finish what I start, beginning at home with my family and with my friends. Amen.

10

Jesus Is a Friend Who Is Wise

Of all the qualities we have studied in this book, wisdom has to be one of most important to look for in a friend. Why? I don't know about you, but most of my friends make as many mistakes as I do! So, it's nice to have a friend like Jesus, who shows us the way and helps us learn how to make better choices.

Jesus again shows us the way. His entire life is a perfect example of wisdom. Who better to teach us about wisdom than Jesus, the wisest person who ever lived? In fact, Jesus *is* wisdom. As God, He had perfect knowledge. Therefore, He did everything with perfect wisdom. And when Jesus was on earth, He made all the right choices. It's nice to have a friend like this, isn't it?

What is wisdom? It is seen in...

the choices you make,

the actions you take, and

the words you speak.

That's what true wisdom is. All summed up, wisdom is the correct application of knowledge. A good goal for you is to learn how to develop the wisdom you need, the wisdom that makes you more like Jesus—not only in the way you live, but in the decisions you make.

Fun in God's Word!

How can you develop wisdom? Or, put another way, how can you be more like Jesus and make right decisions more often?

To answer these questions, let's look again at the life of Jesus, and especially His wise actions.

Wisdom's starting point is Jesus. From the beginning of this book, we've been talking about being Jesus' friend—and that's exactly where true wisdom begins. From the minute you accept Jesus as your Savior and friend, you take on a new life, the life of your friend Jesus. That's what Nicodemus, a teacher in Israel, learned. He came to Jesus wanting to find out more about Him. What did Jesus tell Nicodemus as he came seeking truth and wisdom?

Jesus replied, "Very truly I tell you, no one can see the kingdom of God unless they are born again" (John 3:3).

What was true of Nicodemus applies to you as well: You must be born again. Wisdom is knowing the God of all wisdom, Jesus.

What two changes occur in your life when you accept Christ as your Savior?

If anyone is in Christ, the new creation has come: The old has gone, the new is here! (2 Corinthians 5:17).

#1 _____

_____

#2 _____

_____

Wisdom's teacher is the Holy Spirit. When Jesus was on the earth, His every action was done with wisdom. He also taught wisdom to the people who heard Him speak. He was *the* ultimate source of wisdom! When Jesus began talking about leaving the disciples, they became very concerned. What did Jesus say He would do so the disciples would not be without His wisdom after He went back to heaven?

When the Advocate [the Holy Spirit] comes, whom I will send to you from the Father—the Spirit of truth who goes out from the Father—he will testify about me (John 15:26).

_____

What was "the Advocate"—the one who will testify about Jesus—called?

Jesus called Him the Spirit of _____

According to the verses that follow, what is the Holy Spirit's mission in the life of a believer?

When he, the Spirit of truth, comes, he will guide you into all the truth (John 16:13).

The Holy Spirit will _____

_____

We continually ask God to fill you with the knowledge of his will through all the wisdom and understanding that the Spirit gives (Colossians 1:9).

The Holy Spirit will give you

_____

Wisdom's handbook is the Bible. You begin walking on the path to true wisdom when Jesus becomes your personal Savior and friend. That's also when you receive the power and guidance and wisdom of the Holy Spirit. But that's not all you need for a life of making right choices. You need the wisdom of Jesus that comes from knowing His Word, the Bible.

What did the psalmist say happens when you read and think about the teachings the Bible gives you?

Oh, how I love your law [the Bible]! I meditate on it all day long. Your commands are always with me and make me wiser than my enemies (Psalm 119:97-98).

Your commands

_____

Your commands

Getting to know Jesus by reading your Bible will give you the knowledge you need to make wise decisions, better choices, and speak with wisdom. Jesus has a plan for your life. As you read your Bible, you grow in wisdom, which prepares you for Jesus' purpose for you.

Wisdom's path requires prayer. Jesus, who was God in human flesh, constantly looked to the Father for wisdom through prayer. What do you see Jesus doing in the Garden of Gethsemane as He prepared to make His way to the cross?

> *Going a little farther [away from His disciples], he fell with his face to the ground and prayed..."My Father...may your will be done"* (Matthew 26:39,42).

Read the instructions Jesus gave about praying in Matthew 7:7. (A good way to remember is to think of the letters A-S-K:)

Ask and it will be given to you;

Seek and you will find;

Knock and the door will be opened to you.

What is the result of A-S-King, according to verse 8?

For everyone who asks receives; the one who seeks finds; and to the one who knocks, the door will be opened.

Those who ask— _____

Those who seek— _____

Those who knock— _____

Read the advice James 1:5 gives about how to get wisdom:

If any of you lacks wisdom, you should ask God, who gives generously to all without finding fault, and it will be given to you.

When should you ask for wisdom?

_____

Who should you ask for wisdom?

_____

How is God described?

_____

_____

What is the promise and the result of asking for wisdom?

_____

_____

Wisdom is available to you when you pray—when you A-S-K. Whatever happens in your day—no matter how bad or crazy things are—ask God for help. Whenever you need to make a decision, stop for a minute and check in with God. A-S-K Him for His help—for His wisdom.

Wisdom's progress is ongoing. Jesus was wisdom in a man's body. He was God. But He chose to allow Himself to progress like other boys while growing up. What does this verse say about Jesus' normal human growth progress—about the four areas in which He grew?

> *Jesus grew in wisdom and stature, and in favor with God and man* (Luke 2:52).

Jesus grew in _____

Jesus grew in _____

Jesus grew in _____

Jesus grew in _____

Jesus grew mentally, spiritually, socially, and in wisdom. And you need to do the same and go through the same growth process Jesus did. Wisdom does not come overnight. But the good news is that you can speed up your progress by setting a goal to get wisdom. How can you make this happen? These verses from the book of Proverbs tell you how it's done. Underline anything that will help you grow and progress in wisdom as modeled by Jesus.

The Reward of Wisdom

Blessed are those who find wisdom, those who gain under-standing, for she is more profitable than silver and yields bet-ter returns than gold (Proverbs 3:13-14).

The Source of Wisdom

The fear of the LORD is the beginning of wisdom (Proverbs 9:10).

The Effort of Finding Wisdom

If you look for [wisdom] as for silver and search for it as for hidden treasure, then you will understand the fear of the LORD and find the knowledge of God (Proverbs 2:4-5).

The Importance of Trusting God's Wisdom

Trust in the LORD with all your heart and lean not on your own understanding; in all your ways submit to him, and he will make your paths straight (Proverbs 3:5-6).

What a Friend You Have in Jesus!

Isn't it great to have a friend like Jesus who is always available to you? Jesus always knows the right thing to do, and He will let you know the right thing to do whenever you seek His advice and A-S-K Him for His wisdom.

Because Jesus was perfect, He made perfect decisions and choices. Sadly, this will not always be true of you. You probably already know that when you try and do things your own way...well, it's not pretty. But when you choose to be Jesus' friend, and seek His advice by reading your Bible, praying for help, and asking your parents, you will find the wisdom you need. You will know it is wisdom because:

You will start seeing life from Jesus' point of view.

You will begin choosing better courses of action.

You will be happy with the results of the wisdom you are applying—and so will the other people in your life.

You will make fewer mistakes, both in your behavior and in your choices. And most important of all,

You will be acting more and more like your friend Jesus.

Jesus Is a Friend Who Is Wise

In this chapter we have had some fun in God's Word. Review again how special your friend Jesus is as you write out the points that show you how to follow Jesus down the path of **wisdom**. (I'll get you started with the first point.)

Wisdom's starting point is Jesus _____

Wisdom's teacher is _____

Wisdom's handbook is _____

Wisdom's path requires _____

Wisdom's progress is _____

Write out one thing you liked, learned, or want to do about growing wiser—just like Jesus.

_____

_____

_____

_____

_____

A prayer to pray—

Lord Jesus, thank You for setting a pattern for me to follow as You grew in wisdom, walked in wisdom, spoke with wisdom, and lived out wisdom. I'm so glad You show me and teach me how to be more wise. Help me to always A-S-K You for wisdom as I make choices. Amen.

Also by Jim George

A Boy After God's Own Heart

You've got a lot going on—school, activities, friends, and life at home. And you're taking on new challenges and opportunities which bring up important questions: How do you handle peer pressure and choose the right kind of friends? What if you're having a hard time doing your homework or getting along with your brothers and sisters? And what should you do when you mess up—especially with your parents or God?

The Bible has the answers to these questions and more. With God's help, you can...

- learn how to make good decisions and great friends
- see the benefits of homework and even chores
- get along better with your parents and other family members
- discover more about the Bible so you can grow closer to God

This book will take you on the most amazing journey you can experience—becoming a boy after God's own heart.

A Boy's Guide to Discovering His Bible

The Bible is an epic book! And it's the most important one you'll ever read.

What sets the Bible apart from all other books? It's from God. Through its many adventures and teachings, God is speaking to you about how He wants you to live.

Maybe you think the Bible is confusing and hard to read. If so, this book is for you. You'll learn...

- both helpful and fun ways to understand your Bible
- how to find the many treasures in God's Word
- what God says will make you smarter and stronger

God has a lot to share with you—dive in and see what He's saying!

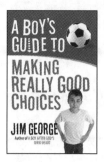

A Boy's Guide to Making Really Good Choices

Did you know that exercising your ability to make good choices is the biggest step you can take toward growing up? That's important because you make lots of decisions every day—

- What should I say…or not say?
- How should I spend my time right now?
- When will I do my schoolwork? My chores?
- Who should I choose as my friends?
- What should I wear…watch…read?

When you make good decisions, you'll do better with God, your parents, your friends, school, and everything else.

So start learning how to make the best kinds of choices…today!

Books by Jim George for Teen Boys

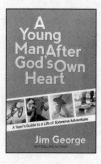

A Young Man After God's Own Heart

Pursuing God really is an adventure—a lot like climbing a mountain. There are all kinds of challenges on the way up, but the awesome view at the top is well worth the trip. This book helps teen guys to experience the thrill of knowing real success in life—the kind that counts with God. (This book was a 2006 Gold Medallion Award Finalist.)

A Young Man's Guide to Discovering His Bible

God's Word can change your life—for real. But that can't happen until you commit yourself to knowing the Bible.

That's what this book by bestselling author Jim George is all about—knowing the Bible, discovering what it says, and making it your personal guide. You'll be surprised how relevant the Bible is in everything you do!

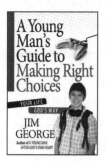

A Young Man's Guide to Making Right Choices

This book will help teen guys to think carefully about their decisions, assuring a more fulfilling and successful life. A great resource for gaining the skills needed to face life's challenges.

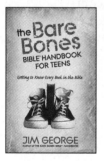

The Bare Bones Bible® Handbook for Teens

Based on the bestselling *Bare Bones Bible® Handbook*, this edition includes content and life application specially written with teens in mind. You will be amazed at how much the Bible has to say about the things that matter the most to you— your happiness, friends and family, home and school, and goals for the future. Great for youth group studies!

To learn more about Harvest House books and
to read sample chapters, visit our website:

www.harvesthousepublishers.com

HARVEST HOUSE PUBLISHERS
EUGENE, OREGON